LINCOLN CHRISTIAN COLLEGE AND SEMINARY

O9-BTO-378

The Practice of Prayer

Prayer

A Guide for Beginners

David Allan Hubbard

InterVarsity Press
Downers Grove
Illinois 60515

First edition © 1972 by David Allan Hubbard under the title
The Problem of Prayer Is . . .
Revised edition © 1983 by David Allan Hubbard

All rights reserved. No part of this book may be
reproduced in any form without written permission from
InterVarsity Press, Downers Grove, Illinois.

InterVarsity Press is the book-publishing division of Inter-Varsity
Christian Fellowship, a student movement active on campus at
hundreds of universities, colleges and schools of nursing.
For information about local and regional activities, write IVCF,
233 Langdon St., Madison, WI 53703.

Distributed in Canada through InterVarsity Press, 860 Denison St., Unit 3,
Markham, Ontario L3R 4H1, Canada.

Cover photograph: Robert Cushman Hayes

ISBN 0-87784-393-7

Printed in the United States of America

Library of Congress Cataloging in Publication Data

Hubbard, David Allan.
    The practice of prayer.

    Reprint. Originally published as: The problem with
prayer is—. Wheaton, Ill.: Tyndale House, 1972.

    1. Prayer.   I. Title.
BV210.2.H77   1983   248.3′2   82-21309
ISBN 0-87784-393-7

12   11   10   9   8   7   6   5   4   3
92   91   90   89   88   87   86   85

111458

111458

Preface

A book on the practice of prayer is a bold venture because prayer itself is the boldest step a human being can take. It is bold—sometimes even brash —to try to know another human being, but it is bolder still to become intimately acquainted with God through prayer. So bold that it seems presumptuous to many.

Prayer is conversation. For example, Psalm 23 begins with God: "He makes me lie down. . . . He leads me; . . . he restores my soul." In the middle of the psalm a change comes. The psalmist no longer talks about God but rather talks to God: "Thou art with me. . . . Thou anointest my head." Here the psalmist begins to pray—confidently.

But prayer is not presumptuous because Jesus Christ prayed and urged us to pray. His example and his command should be our strongest reasons for praying.

What do you want to do in life? Who do you want to be? Do you want to be a sculptor? Then saturate yourself with the works of Michelangelo. Would you like to be a writer of great prose? Then study the works of Samuel Johnson. Is poetry your goal? Then let John Keats be your instructor. Keats was the greatest poet since John Milton. Why was he great? Not because of position; he was an orphan. He was poor all his life. He was sick. He died young. But Keats carried a copy of Milton's *Paradise Lost* with him continually. He soaked himself in the style of a master.

Likewise, do you want to learn to pray? Then listen to Christ as he prayed, "Our Father...."

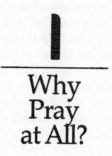

1
Why Pray at All?

PRAYER IS A PROBLEM. We might as well admit it. There are many different reasons, and all of us can find one or more. Many people in our modern society think prayer is an outdated and naive idea, like the saying "every cloud has a silver lining." These people think prayer is a superstitious way of dealing with unknown dangers, of fending off the troubling mysteries of life and of coping with demands too big for us. But all that has changed now because we know so much about life. We have better tools—medicines, appliances. We have better resources—in transportation, in technology. So when problems arise we are more apt to look for help in the yellow pages than in prayer.

Even in churches, prayer is sometimes a ritual or an automatic salute to tradition. We use prayer to round out a service or cap ceremonial occasions such as baby dedications, weddings and funerals.

To some, work has become a substitute for prayer. After all, God expects us to do our best. And we shouldn't use prayer as an excuse to dump responsibilities on God that we ought to carry. "God helps those who help themselves," we chirp as we set out to show God how it should be done.

Talk has also become a substitute for prayer. Even in prayer meetings we often spend more time talking about our problems than praying over them. We use group discussions for problem solving: tensions can be eased, misunderstandings can be cleared up, and relationships can be strengthened if only people can sit face to face and talk, we say.

Then, too, therapy has become a substitute for prayer. Anxiety, depression, hostility—these are problems for professional psychiatrists and psychologists to wrestle with. Why pray when skilled counselors are available to lead us out of our emotional dilemmas into mental freedom and psychic stability?

Please understand that I am not against work or talk or therapy. These are given by God to help us find and express our humanity. But none of these should be a substitute for prayer. Nothing in our modern burgeoning of knowledge, whether technical or behavioral, has made prayer obsolete. Only our misunderstanding of the nature and purpose of prayer makes us think that way.

We need to face honestly some important questions about prayer: What do I say when I pray? How do I know God hears my prayer? What kinds of things should I pray about? How does prayer help us grow? Can I pray about my own problems? What if I don't feel like praying? Can I be honest with God?

Prayer deals with the relationship between an infinite, holy God and his dependent, sinful creatures. Christ and his apostles have told us as much about our relationship to God in prayer as they have about the other great aspects of our faith. And they practiced what they preached.

Why pray at all? Maybe that's the basic question we have to begin with. Prayer does not come easily to most of us. And we can readily ask whether it's worth the struggle.

Obstacles to Praying
To try to identify all the reasons why we do not pray would produce an almost endless catalog. But surely our humanistic way of thinking is one of these obstacles.

The countdown for the launch of Apollo 12 proceeded smoothly as I listened on my car radio. The mammoth rocket, Yankee Clipper, fired on schedule. But no sooner had it lifted off its pad than warning lights began flashing like the scoreboard in the Astrodome. An electrical failure, perhaps caused by lightning, was putting the whole mission and the lives of the astronauts in peril. My first reaction was, "Good thing that the capsule has back-up systems. And those engineers in Mission Control have an ingenuity that's almost legendary." But such thinking was humanistic, secular. Only later did I think to pray.

Our monumental achievements tend to weaken our prayer life. Almost without knowing it, we become victims of a subtle, hidden presumptuousness. Our sense of direct dependence on God can be dulled by our confidence in human ability.

God's sovereignty, strange as it may seem, may also become an obstacle to prayer. After all, since God knows the end from the beginning, who are we to tell him about our needs? He'll work his own will, anyway, won't he? If we are presumptuous to think we don't need God's help, are we not also presumptuous to assume that the sovereign God needs us to help him run the universe?

God's silence is another obstacle to prayer. We often feel like the widow in Christ's parable in Luke 18 who must repeatedly beg the judge to vindicate her cause. Isn't God too busy managing the whole creation to listen to our needs? So why pray?

Our humanistic thinking shows up here as well. We tend to view God as though he were human. We read his silence as an absence of commitment or a loss of interest in us. We find in his refusal to act promptly an indication of lack of concern.

Because we don't really understand the purpose of prayer, we get impatient when we don't see immediate results. We view prayer as a simple transaction: we ask; God answers. We view God as a mail order house—pick a number from the catalog, send it in, two weeks later the doorbell rings, the postman stands at the door with our package, and we open it.

When prayer doesn't work this way, we get edgy with God and quit praying. "I prayed hard about something once," we say, "and God did not pay any attention; so I'm through with prayer."

Reasons for Praying

Despite all we have said about these very real and threatening obstacles, the Bible still presents prayer as an urgent matter, and it gives us good reasons to pray.

God in his sovereignty commands our prayers. Christ's parable of the widow was really a commandment, as the first verse indicates: "And he told them a parable, to the effect that they ought always to pray and not lose heart" (Lk 18:1).

Prayer is our Declaration of Dependence on God, a declaration that needs constant affirmation. Our greatest personal need is simultaneously our toughest problem—depending on God. Since the beginning, we mortals have fought this sense of dependence and defied God's orders. Many have been tempted to live as though there were no God or as though he exists for our benefit. The command to pray is a reminder that we cannot live without God's power, love and guidance.

Prayer is our affirmation of concern for others. It is a beautiful way to obey the command to love our neighbor as ourselves. Biblical love cannot be an act of barter or a mercenary transaction. The purest love is given with no expectation of return. Measured by this standard, earnest prayer for others is a magnificent act of love. Without show or fanfare, we privately, quietly lift the names and needs of others before God's throne. Their concerns have become ours. Their burdens rest on our hearts too. Not that prayer is a substitute for loving deeds; prayer supports and guides the deeds.

God in his compassion responds to our prayers. This is the key to Christ's parable, and it is the second great reason for praying despite the obstacles. Jesus' argument is clear. If a stern judge, who is not moved either by his fear of God or his regard for man, responds to a widow's pleas just because she persists, how much more readily will a compassionate God respond to the cries of his people!

Here we face a mystery. The sovereign God who directs the destinies of peoples and of nations promises to hear and respond to our prayers. This remains a mystery because we are not completely sure how our prayers affect God's sovereignty. Certainly we cannot tell God anything new. Nor can we persuade him to do something he does not want to do. Yet in his majesty and his compassion he demands that we tell him about ourselves, and then he works our prayers into his master plan for our lives.

Isn't this the way we really want it? Prayer reminds us of our constant need for God and reassures us of his presence with us. Prayer is part of God's plan for our growth and for his program in the world. In prayer we don't tell God what to do; we find out what he wants us to do.

This blending of God's sovereignty and compassion that tells us to pray ought to comfort us immensely. In his sovereignty, God knows what is best and does it. In his compassion, God takes our needs and desires into account as he works out his plan.

If a stern, unfeeling judge yields to the plaintive pleading of a widow, how much more will a gracious heavenly Father respond to our prayers. God commands us to pray to minister to our needs. This command, like all his others, is for our good. Prayer is obedience to our omnipotent God; prayer is trust in our loving God. Do we need more reason than that for praying?

Thank you, Father, for sending Jesus to show us what you are like. Your silence when we pray would completely discourage us if he had not shown us your love. Now we know that even your silence is part of your love. We hear your command to pray and your promise to hear. Now that we know who you are, we find it easier to pray. Through Jesus we have learned that dependence on prayer develops our humanity. Forgive our foolish, feverish attempts to hack our way through life without your help. We now know better; help us to do better. For Jesus' sake. Amen.

For further study of related themes refer to the following Scripture passages: Matthew 6:5-8; Luke 11:5-8; 2 Peter 3:9.

2

What
Do I
Say?

PRAYERS COME IN MANY shapes and sizes. The Tibetans, for instance, write their prayers on slips of paper and put them in a great wheel. Each turn of the wheel they count as a recital of their prayer. This mechanized prayer life is rejected by some people who prefer to chant their prayers in dogged repetition. In parts of Mexico Indians make figurines to express their needs—images of corn or cactus or models of their children for whom they are praying. In some cultures prayers are not intelligible sentences but mysterious, magical sounds. The power of the prayer is thought to lie in the uttering of the correct combination of syllables.

How people pray is usually determined by what they believe their deity to be. Look at the manner and content of prayer, and you can tell a great deal about the religious beliefs of the worshipers. Biblical prayer is distinctive in its personal, confident and reverent aspects. Abraham's conversation with God about the pending destruction of Sodom is an example (Gen 18:22-33). He argues as he would with a friend, yet with due regard for God's sovereignty. "Far be it from thee to do such a thing, to slay the righteous with the wicked, so that the righteous fare as the wicked! Far be that from thee! Shall not the Judge of all the earth do right?" (Gen 18:25).

Here Abraham boldly yet reverently pleads a case before God. The nature of his prayer is determined by the character of his God and the nature of the relationship between him and God. No mumbo jumbo, no magic rites, no secret sayings, but open conversation. His beliefs about God shape his prayer, and his prayer is the clear expression of his beliefs. He is convinced that God is both reasonable and righteous, and he prays accordingly. He knows that God is both concerned for human welfare and capable of stern judgment, and this knowledge informs his prayer.

Prayer is a badge of belief. Various Jewish groups had their own ways of praying, their own special expressions that bound them together and marked them off from other groups. This custom is reflected in the request that Jesus' disciples made of their Master: "He was praying in a certain place, and when he ceased, one of his disciples said to

him, 'Lord, teach us to pray, as John taught his disciples' '' (Lk 11:1). Apparently those who followed
John the Baptist were taught special prayers to express their understanding of the faith. Jesus' disciples wanted their own way to voice their new-
found beliefs. Jesus' response came, of course, in
what we call the Lord's Prayer, the badge of Christian discipleship.

What should we say when we pray? If we are
followers of Jesus Christ, we ought to pray along
the lines that he taught his first followers. When we
look at this prayer carefully, we see that it is a means
of maintaining the relationship between us and
God. Our prayer life, then, is based on two things:
God's nature and our needs. In a magnificent way
those are brought together in the Lord's Prayer.
And well they should be, because the one who has
taught us to pray is God become man. He said
about himself, "No one knows the Father except
the Son," and John said about him, "He knew all
men and needed no one to bear witness of man; for
he himself knew what was in man" (Mt 11:27; Jn
2:25).

Prayer as Jesus taught it was a close combination
of basic attitudes and specific elements. What we
affirm or ask for is bound to reflect our attitude
toward God.

Attitudes of Prayer
Words are important, and Jesus taught us to pray
with words. But words are not enough. They must
be framed in a context of fellowship with God.
The disposition of our heart is crucial to this fellow-

ship. In the words which open and close the Lord's Prayer, Jesus makes clear what our attitudes in prayer are to be.

Intimacy is one aspect. "Our Father" is the phrase we use to address God. The Jews were reluctant even to speak God's name, and they often used terms like *The Name*, *Heaven* and *King of the Universe* when they spoke to God. Jesus said, "Call him 'Our Father.' "

The Old Testament used *Father* as a metaphor or simile for God, but not in direct address: "As a father pities his children, so the LORD pities those who fear him" (Ps 103:13). It took the Son's arrival to show us God as Father. "And no one knows the Father except the Son and any one to whom the Son chooses to reveal him" (Mt 11:27).

Because of Jesus, the Son, we can say, "Our Father," and express our intimacy with God. Not that intimacy means lack of respect. The term *Father* is filled with honor and dignity, especially when we go on to say, "Who art in heaven."

Humility as well as intimacy must be the mood of our praying. God is in heaven; we are on earth. There is a lot of difference between those realms. Our Father in heaven is Lord of the kingdom of life and light. He is ruler of the age to come and has been forever. All that we look forward to by faith he already enjoys and always has enjoyed. Heaven's glory and power are commonplace to him. But they are not and can never be to us.

The contrast between God's realm in heaven and ours on earth reminds us constantly of his power and our weakness, of his wisdom and our foolishness, of his wholeness and our inadequacies, of his righteousness and our rebellion. Remember the gap; respect the difference. This is part of what Christ is teaching us about prayer.

Expectation is also a basic attitude that Christ's disciples should have when they pray. The Lord's Prayer was not given to mock us. The things that we are told to pray for are not held tantalizingly beyond our reach. It is our Father to whom we pray. And his aim is not to fool or frustrate us. Because his realm is heaven, he has the perspective to see our needs and the power to meet them.

No wonder the ending of the Lord's Prayer has become so important to us. The one to whom the kingdom, the power and the glory belong is our Father. He will work his will. He will meet our needs. Provision, forgiveness and protection are all beyond our doing but not beyond his.

Elements of Prayer

Expectantly, humbly, intimately we pray to our Father. As we do, we include specific elements that express our relationship with God. We adore his name. We pray for the basic needs of others. As God's children we let him know what we desire. At the same time we acknowledge our sins and beg God for his power and protection.

Adoration is where prayer begins. "Hallowed be thy name" is the phrase which shows the gap between us and God. "I am God and not man, the Holy One in your midst," God once told Hosea (Hos 11:9). The distinction between God and man has been confused ever since Adam and Eve tried

21

to grasp at divinity. When we pray, "Hallowed be thy name," we are acknowledging and celebrating that difference. What can we give God besides our praise? He already owns everything else.

Intercession plays a vital part in prayer, especially on behalf of God's great program for our deliverance. The Lord's Prayer bypasses some of the petty things we are prone to pray for. It focuses on what is really important—God's will and God's kingdom. Certainly we pray for the physical needs of our friends and loved ones. But first in our thoughts and prayers should be our concern that they find their place in God's program and join the company of those whose highest good in life is God's will.

Petition is not to be overlooked. In the heart of the Lord's Prayer is the mention of bread. This is a real world God has put us in. We are not to live by bread alone, but we were certainly not made to live without bread. God made us to enjoy bread, and he made bread for us to enjoy. When we ask God to supply our daily needs, we are saluting two great realities of life: the goodness of God's creation and the constancy of God's care. If we keep these realities in mind, even our petitions become forms of praise.

Confession cannot be omitted from our regular prayer life. The reason is obvious: sin is part of our daily existence. It cuts across the grain of our relationship with God. It violates his will and hinders the progress of his kingdom. God knows all about this sin, of course. The purpose of our confession is for us to let him know that we take seriously our faults and failures. And God also wants us to believe so much in our need for forgiveness that we include in our prayer a pledge to forgive others.

Submission is expressed in our prayer when we ask for strength to stand life's tests and for deliverance from the clutches of the tempter. What do I say when I pray? I ask for forgiveness for sins that I have committed and for power to resist future temptation. I commit myself to God's hands and admit that I cannot deal with life's temptations on my own. His strength, his guidance and his wisdom are what I need. As long as pride and self-confidence trick me into thinking that I am self-sufficient, I am utterly vulnerable to defeat. But submission can lead to victory as I pray for deliverance from the evil one.

Here then is our model prayer, our badge of discipleship. Nowhere else can we learn more about what to say when we pray or how to say it. There are three other points in this prayer which set the pattern for us.

The prayer is *communal*. Throughout we use the plural: our Father, our bread, our debts. These very words encourage us not only to pray alone but to pray with others—friends, neighbors, fellow church members, family. In fellowship we will find strength. In praying with others we will increase the joy and comfort we gain from prayer. And we will demonstrate the fact that we belong not only to God but to his people.

The prayer is *practical*. I stress practical because it deals with our most pressing needs in every area of life. The glory and splendor of God, the success of his program in the lives of his people, our physical needs, the forgiveness of our foolish rebellion, power and poise in the teeth of temptation—what greater issues can we pray about than these?

The prayer is *powerful*. Powerful, indeed! It confronts us with our needs and links us to the glorious God of heaven who alone can deal with them.

Those who do not know our Father in heaven pray in gloom and despair, in fury and frenzy, in weird act and wild ritual. But Christians can pray in hope and in power. No rites or spells, no hexes or witchcraft. In person-to-person conversation, we talk about God's greatness and our needs. Through the merits of Jesus Christ we say, "Our Father who art in heaven." As we do, everything else we need to pray about will fall into place.

Our Father, forgive us for all the other names we are tempted to hallow: friends, family, leaders, heroes, celebrities. Let it be your name alone to which we look for our basic needs. Let it be your will alone around which we build our lives. Let it be your grace alone on which we depend for daily provision. Let it be your power that holds us straight when temptations seek to bend us crooked. It is your Son Jesus who taught us to pray like this. Day by day help us to be good pupils of his. In his name. Amen.

For further study of related themes refer to the following Scripture passages: 1 Kings 18:25-40; Luke 11:2-4; John 17:15; 2 Thessalonians 3:3.

3

Does God
Really
Hear?

NONE OF US HAS had every prayer answered. And
it's a good thing. God often protects us from our
inexperience and brashness by refusing to grant
our requests. We can accept this with a reasonable
amount of good will, but when we ask for things
that we know to be good and find God silent, our
problem deepens. God has sent no acknowledg-
ment to let us know he has received our prayers.
There is silence, stony silence, which sometimes
spawns deep and serious questions about God and
his commitment to us.

Does God care? If God's love is as strong and
constant as the Bible says, why does he allow my

life to be buffeted and battered by harsh circumstances?

Job felt the sting of this question. Shorn of his goods, bereft of his family, rejected by his wife, goaded by his friends, he groped for explanations and found none. He had confidence in his own integrity. He knew he had done nothing to deserve such profound suffering. Yet he could not conclude that God had abandoned him, so he suffered on, wondering about God's love.

Is God fair? If God loves justice as the Bible declares, why is life so filled with injustice? Wickedness seems to roll on unchecked, while righteousness is stalled in its tracks or detoured to the back roads of life.

Good and wise people in biblical days puzzled over this question, especially the prophet Habakkuk. In a remarkable conversation with God, he pointedly told God that "the law is slacked and justice never goes forth. For the wicked surround the righteous, so justice goes forth perverted" (Hab 1:4). When God finally broke his silence, Habakkuk was more vexed than ever. God promised to discipline his people by sending the Babylonians to ravage their land. Habakkuk's protest was powerful: "Thou who art of purer eyes than to behold evil and canst not look on wrong, why dost thou look on faithless men, and art silent when the wicked swallows up the man more righteous than he?" (Hab 1:13). These are pressing questions whenever God seems to turn his back on his people.

Is God able? If he has all the power with which

he is credited, why do the events of life become so disordered? Why does he not intervene? We feel like the disciples in the boat with Jesus during the storm. Our lives are in danger, and our Master seems asleep.

These questions about God's silence were known to Jesus. To deal with them he urged his disciples to pray—to pray regularly, fervently, expectantly. "Ask, and it will be given you; seek, and you will find; knock, and it will be opened to you" (Mt 7:7). Silence there may be, but God's silence does not mean abandonment. Rather, it means he is still listening.

Confidence in Our Relationship

The high privileges of sonship—this is where Jesus comes down hard. Prayer is conversation between God's children and their heavenly Father. It is our confidence in this relationship that makes prayer possible even when we have no immediate evidence that God is hearing us.

This relationship is not magical. In many cultures both ancient and modern, people have tried to break God's silence by magical rites or spells. If what they have prayed for does not come to pass, they may try another witchdoctor, sacrifice another chicken or chant a different formula. For them, getting answers to their prayers is a matter of manipulation, of discovering the proper ceremony, of reciting the correct phrases.

This relationship is *not mystical.* Our firm confidence that God will hear our prayer is not based on secret information any more than on magical practice. Because we are God's children through Jesus Christ, we do not resort to spell or hex or witchcraft when we want God's attention. Nor do we base our prayers on mystical feelings about our relationship to God. Feelings we do have, and they are important. But whether we pray and what we pray for are issues too important to be put at the mercy of anything as fickle as our feelings. We are to make our needs known to God whether we feel like it or not.

This relationship is *historical*. That is the message of the Bible. Our sonship, which gives us the privilege to talk to God and the confidence that he hears, is not based on our ability to manipulate him by magic or to outguess him by mystical intuition. Our sonship is based on what God has done in history through Jesus and our personal acceptance of Christ as our Savior.

How do I know God hears my prayer? Because Jesus has shown me what God is like. Even when the answer does not come in my time or on my terms, he has given me reasons not to doubt. His silence may not be pleasant, but it is not overwhelming because of his clear reassurance through Jesus Christ.

The questions that normally would haunt us have been answered by the great deeds of Jesus. Does God care? The whole life of Jesus answers a resounding yes! God cares much more about us than we care about our children, and we know the deep concerns we have for them. We are sensitive to their needs, committed to their welfare, hurt by their failures, cheered by their growth. And our love can scarcely compare with God's.

Jesus does more than talk about God's love; he demonstrates it on the cross. "For God so loved the world that he gave his only Son" (Jn 3:16) is the message of the gospel. Even God's silence, his seeming reluctance to answer our prayer, cannot cancel that great reality. God does care. That is the message written in blood on the cross.

The cross also tells us that God is fair. Justice as well as love speaks from the cross. God, who is "faithful and just to forgive our sins," is just in all he does. Our sin required punishment. God saw to it that justice was done, though it cost him separation from his Son.

The cross also speaks to the other question that God's silence is apt to raise: Is God able? Simply put, the answer from the cross is that the God who has the power to save us from our deepest problem, sin, surely can cope with all lesser tests.

This relationship is *personal* as well as historical. Our sonship, our intimate relationship with God, is grounded in what God has said and done through Jesus: his teachings, his death, his resurrection. This historical base is absolutely fundamental. If God had not done this saving work through Jesus, our prayer would be futile because we would not be his children with free access to his presence and power.

To experience God's love, justice and power when he is silent, we must see ourselves in the Bible. When we read about his caring for people and giving them rest and comfort, we must see ourselves. The widow whose faithfulness he honored, the little children whom he blessed, the crooked

29

tax collector who became an honest man through faith, the religious leader whose daughter was healed by Jesus—these people we become by taking God at his word.

Commitment to Share This Grace

"If you then, who are evil, know how to give good gifts to your children, how much more will your Father who is in heaven give good things to those who ask him!" (Mt 7:11). This is the way Jesus sums up our relationship to our heavenly Father. He is good and great; we can trust him for everything.

This passage drives on to a conclusion which may surprise us: "So whatever you wish that men would do to you, do so to them; for this is the law and the prophets" (Mt 7:12). The grand promise of prayer is followed immediately by the golden rule of love. The vertical relationship of spiritual sonship requires the horizontal expression of brotherhood. Our life from God must be channeled to the needs of people.

One way for us to keep our perspective when God seems silent is to occupy ourselves with the lives of others. In doing this we rise above our feelings. God's love for us on the cross stands tall in the midst of our circumstances, however grim they seem, and testifies to God's care. God has been utterly, matchlessly, finally good to all who trust him through his Son. Therefore the golden rule is always in effect for his followers.

Job, Habakkuk and the disciples of Jesus discovered that God's faithfulness, love and power eventually break his silence and bring his answer.

But his love and power are at work even in the silence. Our inheritance is based on what Jesus has done for us, and nothing can change that. How do I know God hears my prayers? He has promised to hear the prayers of his children. Jesus said it plainly: we are to seek, knock and ask, and God will reveal, open and answer.

Our Father, teach us the simple lessons of sonship, the basic courses in asking and receiving. Teach us especially the "patience of unanswered prayer." We rest in your love because you have made it so clear in Jesus. We trust your sense of fairness because we know that the Judge of all the earth does right. We bank on your power because you have solved our greatest problem when you accepted us in Jesus. Help us to remember that the asking is our business and the answering is yours. Through Jesus Christ, your Son, our Lord, we pray. Amen.

For further study of related themes refer to the following Scripture passages: Luke 11:9-13; Mark 11:24; John 15:7; 16:23-24; 1 John 3:22-24; 5:14-15.

4

Can I Pray about My Problems?

THERE IS NO MERIT in timidity where prayer is involved. Timidity and reverence are not synonymous. Some of the finest saints in the Bible prayed with boldness, almost brashness.

Almost half of the psalms are complaints of individuals. Passionately, eloquently, fervently, they pour out their hearts to God. Their needs vary. Sometimes they are being accused of a crime and want to protest the charges. At other times they are suffering physical illness and the torture of abandonment by friends and family who, like Job's friends, are sure that the illness is punishment for sin.

Still others are conscience stricken over their sins and long for forgiveness to clear their account with God. Some have enemies stalking their paths, trying to do them in. Whatever the plight that prompts the psalmist to pray, these psalms all have one thing in common—a direct, open, bold, personal plea for help.

Prayer for others should be the basic burden of our prayer life. For Christians, love is the law of life. We have been captured by the love that God showed us in Christ when he entered our human plight and brought meaning to it. This love is to be shared, not hoarded. Prayer for others is one of the best ways of loving.

When we pray for others we offer them the highest service by treating them with such great dignity that we voice their needs before the throne of the King of the universe. We affirm their personal worth by taking time and energy to seek their welfare before the court of heaven. We encourage God to meet their needs, to let his power work on their behalf for their good and his glory.

These prayers are acts of love and should set the style of our prayer life for others. But prayer as an expression of love prompts the question, "Can I pray about *my own* problems?"

The prayers of the Bible show us the answer is yes. And they give us good examples of how this is done without letting our prayers deteriorate into selfish whines. A psalm of lament such as Psalm 143 shows us that we can bring our own needs to God in confidence. It also shows us the context of faith and commitment within which we do this.

Dependence on God's Help

Prayer for our own needs can be an act of discipleship. The experience of our psalmist makes this clear. "Let me hear in the morning of thy steadfast love, for in thee I put my trust. Teach me the way I should go, for to thee I lift up my soul" (Ps 143:8). In the midst of his problems, this man of faith declares his dependence on God's help. Enemies are making life miserable for him, perhaps seeking to take his life. Yet he puts his trust in God.

And his attitude remains positive despite his plight. He pleads without chiding; he asks without blaming. Not his own merit, but God's greatness is his hope. He makes no claim to righteousness, but casts himself on God's mercy: "Enter not into judgment with thy servant; for no man living is righteous before thee" (v. 2). He knows he has no other refuge. So trustingly and fervently he makes his needs known to God.

Affirmation of God's Character

The psalmist's petitions, and ours, are based more on who God is than on what we need. The verses of this prayer are dotted with references to God and what he is like. This keeps the psalmist from stewing in his suffering, as his prayer becomes an affirmation of God's character.

God's faithfulness is what the psalmist mentions first. "Hear my prayer, O LORD; give ear to my supplications! In thy faithfulness answer me" (v. 1). "Dependability" is the best way to explain faithfulness; God never lets us down.

Unless we believe this, we dare not pray. If God

cannot be depended on, we are in trouble whether he answers our prayer or not. If he answers it, how do we know it is an answer which is good for us? If he does not answer it, maybe it is because he is not able. Then where are we?

God's *righteousness* along with God's faithfulness can ease our anxiety just at this point. We not only can depend on God, we can depend on him to do the right thing for us. This is important because we can never be fully sure that we are asking for the right things in the right way and with the right motives. We have been sinners since Adam, and sinners we shall remain through this life. It is good to remember that even our prayers are vulnerable to sin. But we can trust God's righteousness. He will protect us not only from our problems but from our foolish prayers in the midst of our problems. "In thy righteousness bring me out of trouble!" is the way our psalmist puts his prayer (v. 11). He has confidence in God's power and at the same time is willing to commit himself to God's solution.

God's *steadfast love* looms large in the mind of this man of Israel, along with God's faithfulness and righteousness. His suffering is not only exasperating, it is excruciating. "For the enemy has pursued me; he has crushed my life to the ground; he has made me sit in darkness like those long dead. Therefore my spirit faints within me; my heart within me is appalled" (vv. 3-4). He keeps going by his knowledge that God still loves him and will see him through. "Let me hear in the morning of thy steadfast love" (v. 8); and again, "And in thy steadfast love cut off my enemies" (v. 12).

God's pledge of loyalty to his people gives the writer courage and confidence to pray for his own problems. Even in his suffering—especially in his suffering—he does not lose sight of the unique relationship that God has formed with his people. He prays not as a stranger but as one who belongs, not as an outsider but as a member of God's family, not as an enemy of God but as one bound to God by loyal love.

Faithful, righteous, steadfast in love, the God of the psalmist welcomes this personal prayer because it affirms his character. It is free from bitterness, self-righteousness and despair. Its faith rings true in the grip of suffering.

Meditation on God's Deeds

How does the psalmist know what God is like? Where did he gain these insights into God's goodness and grace? From meditation on God's deeds, says the poet. "I remember the days of old, I meditate on all that thou hast done; I muse on what thy hands have wrought" (v. 5).

Without this perspective from the past, the present seems to overwhelm us. We stand so close to our problems that sometimes we cannot see beyond them. The sharpness of our pain drowns out the assurance of God's power. Think on the deeds of God; remember all he has done. Look at the exodus from Egypt, the cross of Calvary, the empty garden tomb. This is the reminder we need when life tries to shake us apart.

"Faith comes from what is heard, and what is heard comes by the preaching of Christ" (Rom

10:17). As we pray about our personal problems, nothing will help us more than hearing what Christ has done for us. Assertions of his power and love fuel the fires of our faith. And as our faith brightens, our doubts cool to manageable temperatures.

There is no magic in preaching or reading the Bible, but there is spiritual power that can draw our thoughts away from our weakness and connect them to God's purposes. Our petitions about personal concerns need not be gasped in hollow tones of despair; they can be voiced in faith and confidence when we remember what God has done for us.

Dedication to God's Program

At its heart, prayer is humble pleading. It is an act of surrender. Our meditation on God's great deeds in the past calls us to dedicate ourselves to God's program. This is exactly what happened to the psalmist.

Devotion to God's will is part of what he demonstrates. "Teach me to do thy will, for thou art my God!" (Ps 143:10). Neither self-righteous nor self-pitying, this man of prayer knows that there are lessons of obedience yet to be learned. His prayer deliberately leans away from presumptuousness. His task is not to teach God how to answer the prayer; his aim is to learn from God at whatever cost.

Concern for God's name is also part of his remarkable dedication. "For thy name's sake, O LORD, preserve my life!" (v. 11). Here is the ultimate weapon to ward off selfishness in prayer. Not our need, but God's name is our basic concern.

This is exactly what Jesus had in mind when he taught us to begin our prayers, "Our Father who art in heaven, hallowed be thy name" (Mt 6:9).

Commitment to be God's servant is the final act of dedication. "And in thy steadfast love cut off my enemies, and destroy all my adversaries, for I am thy servant" (Ps 143:12). This bold prayer flows from the psalmist's special relationship with God. As God's servant he is part of God's household, confident of special privileges. He is obligated to serve God and is sure that God has obligated himself to protect him. As God's servant he has a claim on God, yet he voices this claim humbly. The psalmist is mindful that he takes orders from God, not vice versa.

Can you pray about your own problems? You can if the psalmist's spirit has rubbed off on you.

His predicament has not forced him to bitterness. Easing his pain and comforting his distress is the conviction that God knows what is best and will do it.

His boldness does not turn to insolence. With all his forcefulness and directness, his attitude remains reverent. He has not let his dire predicament blind him to the greatness of God.

His concern for himself does not degenerate into selfishness. He is preoccupied with God. With fervor he makes his cause known, yet he stands ready to bend to God's good will and to guard God's good name.

Whatever your problems, pray about them. Whatever pressures weigh you down, drop them before your heavenly Father. Not in anxiety but in confidence, pray. Not in bitterness about the present but in openness to God's good future, pray. Not in rebellion toward your circumstances but in surrender to his will, pray. Let God's goodness and glory be your confidence and your concern, and then pray what you will. God will do the rest.

Thank you, Father, for teaching us to pray. And thank you for your patience as we learn. We can certainly identify with the psalmist's plight. Help us also to identify with his faith and dedication. We want no part of selfishness masquerading as piety. Years ago we learned to sing, "Trust and obey, for there's no other way." Now lead us to live like that too. Through Jesus Christ who made it possible. Amen.

For further study of related themes refer to the following Scripture passages: Luke 22:39-46; Job 23:1-17; Psalms 141—142.

5

What More Is There to Pray For?

SELFISHNESS IS NEVER pretty, even in prayer. It is easy for us to be caught up in our own needs and try to use God as a mail order house. "Please give me this." "I must have that." "Enclosed find a list of the things my family and I need before Christmas."

The Bible encourages us to make our needs known to God, but a prayer life limited to personal, tangible needs is evidence that our Christian outlook does not perceive our deepest needs and God's grandest gifts. Our prayers for others may also be shortsighted. We can become preoccupied with their material needs and limit our concern to matters of their health and comfort. As important as these are, they should not hold a monopoly on our prayer time.

If prayer for others is one way to show our love, then our prayer for others ought to deal with the deepest, most pressing needs that others have. What kinds of things do I pray about? How do I move beyond selfishness in prayer? How do I focus on really important requests so that I pray more and more according to God's will?

One suggestion is to follow the example of the apostle Paul. In several of his letters he opens with a prayer for his readers. In addition he often breaks spontaneously into prayer so that the pages of his letters are sprinkled with intercession to God. In the middle of 1 Thessalonians, for instance, Paul pushes his thoughts heavenward: "Now may our God and Father himself, and our Lord Jesus, direct our way to you; and may the Lord make you increase and abound in love to one another and to all men, as we do to you, so that he may establish your hearts unblamable in holiness before our God and Father, at the coming of our Lord Jesus with all his saints" (3:11-13).

This is intercession at its best. The deep, basic needs of his friends are brought before God. The highest, brightest purposes of God in their lives are sought: an increase of love and holiness.

Though Paul wrote to the Colossians from prison in Rome, his thoughts are not so much of himself as of them. The contrast is sharp and bold. For himself he asks one thing—and that at the very end of the letter: "Remember my fetters" (Col 4:18). For them Paul writes four chapters of instruction in Christian growth. He even includes a prayer for them by Epaphras, their pastor, who is with Paul in Rome: "Epaphras, who is one of yourselves, a servant of Christ Jesus, greets you, always remembering you earnestly in his prayers, that you may stand mature and fully assured in all the will of God" (4:12).

Paul makes his own concerns for them clear in the first chapter where he voices one of the powerful prayers of the Bible. "And so, from the day we heard of it [your love in Christ], we have not ceased to pray for you, asking that you may be filled with the knowledge of his will in all spiritual wisdom and understanding" (1:9).

Pray for Insight
What kinds of things should we pray about? Pray that those you know and love may have spiritual insight. Here we are asking God to grapple with our deepest human problem—our inability to grasp his truth. This was one of Paul's chief concerns. Listen to his words in Ephesians: "Now this I affirm and testify in the Lord, that you must no longer live as the Gentiles do, in the futility of their minds; they are darkened in their understanding, alienated from the life of God because of the ignorance that is in them, due to their hardness of heart" (4:17-18). Again, he exhorts the Romans: "Be transformed by the renewal of your mind, that you may prove what is the will of God" (Rom 12:2).

The aim of this insight is to know the will of God. This is just what our darkened minds find hard to do. Mathematics we can learn; chemistry we can fathom; recipes and knitting instructions we can understand. But sin affects us most in obscuring the will of God.

When we pray that our friends will have insight into God's will, we do not mean that they will know exactly what to do in every decision they face. God's will, as Paul understands it, is his program and purposes for his people. We need insight into the great goals that God has for his own—our maturity in Christ and our partnership in God's mission. To be in God's will means taking my place in God's grand plan for making his name known to the world. When this larger issue is settled, the details of day-to-day living tend to fall into place.

This is a great prayer, an exquisite act of love— to pray that those we care about will be caught up in the noble purposes of God. Then they will be freed for growth and discipleship.

The result of this insight is to live a life pleasing to God. Let's hear again how Paul puts it in his own prayer: "That you may be filled with the knowledge of his will in all spiritual wisdom and understanding, to lead a life worthy of the Lord, fully pleasing to him, bearing fruit in every good work and increasing in the knowledge of God" (Col 1:9-10). This insight into God's will is practical as well as idealistic. God shares his program and opens his secrets to us not just to thrill our souls but to change our lives.

As the Bible looks at life, theory and practice, knowledge and action, go hand in hand. If our knowledge does not produce changed character, it is not true knowledge. We pray that our loved ones may have insight into God's way of salvation and their part in it. When we pray this way, we are also praying that their lives will be so transformed that what they say and do will shine with that same love of God that "drew salvation's plan." This life of love is pleasing to God, and love itself is the fruit we are to bear by God's help. Insight is needed if we are to understand God's love and commit ourselves to live by love.

Pray for Power

I should also pray that lives intertwined with mine shall be given power to cope with the problems that life throws at them. God's work of saving people and our work of sharing his love go on in a world of selfishness, hate, apathy and rebellion. No wonder Paul prays for power.

The measure of this power is God himself. "May you be strengthened with all power, according to his glorious might" (Col 1:11). Power was something the ancient peoples knew about. Their superstitions traced power to magic, to the forces of the universe, to the pagan priests who practiced sorcery and witchcraft. The enemies of the Christian faith tried to employ these powers against those who had met God in Jesus Christ and been transferred from the kingdom of darkness to the kingdom of light. But this pagan power was no match for God's. Resurrection, not superstition, is the way God demonstrated his power. We can bank on it.

The purpose of this power is our endurance with

joy and thanksgiving. Those for whom we pray need both insight and power. Ignorance and weakness are dominant, inescapable human traits. And life has a way of taking advantage of us on both counts. It tricks us where we are ignorant and exploits us where we are weak. Power to endure affliction is what Paul prays for. And all of us need that. Life rubs us the wrong way frequently, especially when we go against the world's grain by trying to be consistently Christian. But God's power helps us to bear up and to be patient.

Endurance and patience are the outstanding results produced by God's power. But even more, there can be joy in the teeth of affliction. When we really know God and are anchored to his love, nothing the world does can shake that relationship. Joy is that quality of confidence and poise which we have because the real issues of life are settled—and settled in our favor.

Despite circumstances that could defeat or discourage us, we can give thanks. The outcome of God's program is assured. Only victory lies ahead. This knowledge helps us to take life as it comes, with joy and gratitude.

What kinds of things do I pray about? Let's take a clue from Paul's prayer: insight into God's will and power to do it in all circumstances. Note the boldness of this prayer. Paul seeks great things from God and in generous portions. "That you may be filled with the knowledge of his will [and knowledge can be translated "full knowledge"] in all spiritual wisdom . . . fully pleasing to him, bearing fruit in every good work . . . strengthened with all power . . . for all endurance and patience with joy."

Because his cause is right and his motives are sound, Paul prays boldly. He knows God is able. He has lavish confidence in God's power and good will.

Paul's boldness is braced by God's strong works of salvation which are the basis of this prayer. Paul's final thoughts are not of the needs of his friends but of the deeds of God through his beloved Son, "in whom we have redemption, the forgiveness of sins" (Col 1:14). Without these acts of God's grace, our prayer would be wishful thinking, idle meditation. But God has acted on our behalf, and we can ask on behalf of those we love.

Note the connection between Paul's prayer and the one Jesus taught his disciples. "Thy kingdom come/Thy will be done,/On earth as it is in heaven" (Mt 6:10). Insight into God's will and his power to carry it out are the most urgent needs of the human family. Our prayers for each other are part of God's plan for getting his will done. Physical and financial needs are important; we should not forget them. But we should also make sure that our priorities in prayer follow the priorities of God. What higher favor can we do for others than to lift their names before God asking him to catch them up in his plan and to give them a share in carrying it out. To know God and enjoy him forever is our chief purpose. It is that purpose which must permeate our prayers.

Our Father, redemption and forgiveness are your great gifts. Teach us to share the joy of those gifts in prayer. Forgive us when we betray our friends and family by praying only for the incidental and the temporary. We know the permanent things are faith, hope and love. Let our prayers be filled with them. We want your best for ourselves and others. Lead us to express these high desires in prayer day after day. Through Jesus Christ. Amen.

For further study of related themes refer to the following Scripture passages: Isaiah 45:9-13; John 6:38-40; Romans 9:14-26; Ephesians 1:7-10, 15—2:2; 1 Thessalonians 4:1-4.

6

I Don't
Understand
How It Works

A TRAGIC NEWS STORY stunned West Coast readers.
A thirteen-year-old girl had been held prisoner in
her home all her life. Cut off from contacts with the
outside world, she mumbled sounds but could not
talk. She still wore diapers, and her intellectual age
was about two years old. Stunted by isolation and
malnutrition, she could scarcely walk and was skit-
tish in the presence of people. Hopefully, doctors
say, she'll be able to make significant physical and
mental progress in a few years with good care and
training. Her story reminds us how important
growth is, and how much we take it for granted.

Much of our emotional, intellectual, spiritual

and even physical development comes from our association with other people. As children, we hear others talk and we imitate their speech and gestures. We play with older children and absorb the skills and rules of the games almost without knowing it. As grownups we engage in stimulating conversation or hear a provocative talk and thereby stretch our minds. Thinking, choosing, working, loving, praying—these and other human abilities are learned from people around us.

This fact frightened Jesus' disciples when he began to speak of leaving them. For three years they had gone where he went and stayed where he stayed. He was the teacher and they were his pupils, which is what the word *disciple* literally means.

Through their many months of constant contact with the Master, they had grown in understanding of God's will and in confidence toward God's program. Now their Lord and Teacher was to leave them. You can imagine how disturbed they were. No wonder Jesus had to reassure them: "Let not your hearts be troubled; believe in God, believe also in me" (Jn 14:1).

Jesus not only reassured them that they would be all right; he encouraged them that they would be even better off. "Truly, truly, I say to you, he who believes in me will also do the works that I do; and greater works than these will he do, because I go to the Father" (Jn 14:12). They were worried about survival; Jesus promised them growth. They were afraid their whole enterprise would collapse; Jesus predicted that it would thrive.

To illustrate the growth he had in mind, Jesus

used a word picture familiar to all the people of his country. "I am the vine, you are the branches. He who abides in me, and I in him, he it is that bears much fruit, for apart from me you can do nothing" (Jn 15:5). Jesus' friends were acquainted with the Old Testament analogy of God's people as a vine. "Thou didst bring a vine out of Egypt; thou didst drive out the nations and plant it" (Ps 80:8). The vine here is obviously Israel, rescued from Egypt in the exodus and settled in Canaan by the providence of God.

Again, in a poignant song Isaiah pictures Israel as a vine chosen and planted by God. Yet when God went to look for fruit, he found wild grapes. "For the vineyard of the LORD of hosts is the house of Israel, and the men of Judah are his pleasant planting; and he looked for justice, but behold, bloodshed; for righteousness, but behold, a cry!" (Is 5:7). Justice and righteousness were the fruits God desired from Israel, but he found murder and oppression.

Israel, God's vine, chosen by him to bear fruit. This is the background for Jesus' words about growth and fruitfulness. As the vine, Jesus is the new Man of God, the true Servant, wholly committed to do God's will. All who by faith are linked to him are branches of this vine, part of God's people, members of the New Israel, rescued from sin, chosen for service.

The language to describe this relationship may seem strange. In the midst of Jesus' talk of leaving, he begins to stress "abiding," "remaining." "I'll go away, and yet we'll still be together. I will be with you and you with me." You can almost see the disciples' eyes light up with hope as they hear these words. Growth is possible. They will not be cut adrift by Christ and left to wither on their own. They are tied to him, grafted into him. All that his life has meant to them will continue to be theirs when he is gone. Teaching and correction, nurture and comfort, guidance and encouragement—all these will be abundant as Jesus abides in them and they in him.

Vital to Fellowship

He in them and they in him—or, to make it more personal, he in us and we in him. This is a relationship which is difficult to illustrate. A red-hot poker in a blazing fire is one example. The poker is in the fire, and the fire is in the poker. Christ's illustration of branches growing in a vine is much more apt.

The life and energy from the vine courses through the branches, while the branches are knit into the tissue of the vine. The truth that underlies this illustration is not just horticultural; it is personal. Jesus means that our lives are wrapped up in his and his in ours. Our relationship is closer than flesh and blood ties, so close that we become part of each other.

This fellowship, this union, this intimate association is enhanced and enriched by prayer. Fellowship among people is dependent on conversation, and the cruelest blow we can inflict on each other is icy silence. Not to talk is to annihilate other people by treating them as though they did not exist. Quarreling, bickering, insulting, chiding, threatening are not pleasant forms of communication, but they are preferable to relentless silence.

What we say to Christ may not always be pretty or pleasing, but talk to him we must. Our health depends on it. No fellowship—no growth. It's just that simple.

How does prayer help us grow? Our prayer *expresses our commitment to Christ.* By talking to God we reaffirm our basic decision to depend on him. We are protected from our foolishness and steadied in our waywardness as we regularly remember whom we belong to and what we are called to be. "Prone to wander, Lord, I feel it; prone to leave the God I love" is more than a line from a hymn. It is a summary of our lives. There is nothing automatic about abiding in Christ. We need to keep in touch with him regularly. He speaks to us through his Word (Jn 15:7), and we respond in our prayers.

Our prayer *opens us to hear his words.* We are besieged by words in our society. Billboards blaze them into our minds as we drive. Headlines scream from the newspapers. Our phones ring incessantly as people pour out their feelings. Radio and television use sweet, seductive words to coax us to purchase things we don't need at prices we can't afford to pay. Pseudophilosophers and selfish politicians twist our minds to support their points of view. At times it seems that our very sanity is being assailed.

In the midst of all this, we need to shut out the din and hear the better words of Jesus Christ. Regular prayer builds into our lives those experiences of silence and concentration when the still, small voice of our Savior can cut through life's howl and speak his words of peace and joy.

Basic to Obedience

Our fellowship with Christ is a demanding business. Even more than marriage, motherhood or military duty, fellowship with Christ draws the best out of us.

Christ promised to be with his disciples not just to bring them comfort but to help them keep his commandments. This is the fruit Jesus keeps mentioning. "As the branch cannot bear fruit by itself, unless it abides in the vine, neither can you, unless you abide in me.... By this my Father is glorified, that you bear much fruit, and so prove to be my disciples" (Jn 15:4, 8). Fruit in Scripture almost always stands for actions and character traits that God approves. Isaiah's song of the vineyard made this clear. God looked for justice and righteousness as fruit from his vineyard, instead he found wild grapes—bloodshed and oppression. Paul, too, described character traits as fruit in his famous list of "fruit of the Spirit" in Galatians 5. First and foremost he listed love.

Paul got this priority from Jesus. "If you keep my commandments, you will abide in my love, just as I have kept my Father's commandments and abide in his love.... This is my commandment, that you love one another as I have loved you" (Jn 15:10, 12).

Abiding in Jesus means we can be fruitful because his power and love make us so. Being fruitful stems from keeping his commandments. And his commandments center in love.

To sum up—our growth in Jesus is growth in love. How does prayer help us grow? In prayer we recognize our inability to love in our own strength. Frankly, openly, desperately we seek God's help. More than anything else we want to be loving. Yet here more than anywhere else we find ourselves failing.

In prayer we remember Christ's example of love. Prayer helps to black out the false patterns of love which surround us. Prayer shines the spotlight on the life of love that Jesus demonstrated: love that cares, that costs, that gives; love that washes feet and endures wounds.

In prayer we receive Christ's power. Sin and love are bitter enemies. Daily we struggle to defeat the sinfulness that makes love so hard to come by. But our effort is no match for our own selfishness or anybody else's. Christ's power is adequate. His love frees us for love. His presence with us gives us courage and energy to keep his commandments— and the greatest of them is love.

Father, this is the growth we desire. To be tall or smart or rich are not really important to us. But to love is. Deep inside we know that the life of love is the life for us. We hate the selfishness that stunts our growth. We despise the isolation that keeps us undernourished. We detest the arrogance that tempts us to carry on life without Christ. Link us to that chain of love that binds you to Christ and Christ to us. Teach us so to abide in him that we can really pray, and so to pray that we can truly abide. In his great name. Amen.

For further study of related themes refer to the following Scripture passages: Matthew 7:7; John 6:48-58; 16:22-24; James 1:5; 1 John 2:4-6.

7
I Don't Feel Like Praying

PRAYING RARELY COMES easily for us—despite the fact that we were made to pray. Birds don't seem to struggle to muster up a song. Frogs need little exhortation to stir up their croaking. Dogs will bark at the slightest provocation. But prayer, which should be just as normal for men and women as singing is for birds, is hard to come by.

The obvious reason for this is our sin. In the beginning man and woman talked with God as naturally as they breathed. God met Adam and Eve in the cool of the evening and their conversation delighted them. Their rebellion changed all this. Guilty over their disobedience, edgy over their ambition, chagrined at their failure, uncertain of God's concern, Adam and Eve hid from God. Conversation with their Creator was the last thing they wanted at that moment.

And we have shied away from conversation with God ever since. We may pray on occasion, at a civic ceremony, for instance, or when we find ourselves in despair or danger. But much of the time we do not feel like praying. Perhaps God is far from our thoughts, or we may fear what God would say to us should we start to talk to him. Apathy, anger, fear, skepticism—all of these attitudes urge us to retreat from God rather than to open ourselves to him.

These feelings are not limited to people who oppose God's ways. Men and women of faith are not yet free from them. They too have often found it difficult to pray. "What if I don't feel like praying?" Well, you are in distinguished company.

The sturdy prophet Elijah had moments when he did not feel like praying. Jezebel, Ahab's wicked queen, had vowed to take Elijah's life. "But he himself went a day's journey into the wilderness, and came and sat down under a broom tree; and he asked that he might die, saying, 'It is enough; now, O LORD, take away my life; for I am no better than my fathers.' And he lay down and slept under a broom tree" (1 Kings 19:4-5). No hours of petition; no patient waiting for the voice of God; just a gasp of self-pity and a sentence of despair, then sleep. That's Elijah's experience—often like ours.

Jesus' disciples also had their problems with prayer. They had gone out with their Master to the Mount of Olives, a favorite retreat of Jesus. Here, away from the crowds that pressed on him in the city, he could give himself to prayer and meditation. The lamps and torches of Jerusalem flickered dimly in the distance. The towers of David's great capital were stark silhouettes in the moonlight. Yet the scene was far from peaceful on this particular night. Trouble was brewing. A plot was hatching. Jewish priests and Roman rulers had their heads together: murder was on their minds. All this Jesus knew as he led his friends up the winding trail to the spot beneath the gnarled olive trees where he liked to pray.

This time he urged them to pray too. The grim plot that threatened him would not leave them unscathed. Judas had already joined their enemies. And Jesus had predicted that Peter's courage would fail when the showdown came. So the Master virtually commanded his followers to pray: "Pray that you may not enter into temptation" (Lk 22:40). Then he went off a little way by himself; and while he prayed, the disciples slept.

The Disciples' Carelessness

At the moment when prayer should have been on their minds, it seemed beyond them. Apparently they did not feel like praying. There may have been many reasons why: fatigue from the rigors of a difficult day; uncertainty as to what they should pray about; lack of leadership among them to organize their time of prayer. But whatever their reasons, the story is quite clear that they were careless about prayer; they should have prayed, and they did not. Perhaps from their reluctance to pray in time of need we can learn something about our own.

Pangs of failure in their relationship to Christ may have kept them from praying. They did not understand all this talk about his death and what it would accomplish. When he spoke of his power, his kingdom and his glory, they thought in earthly, political terms. They responded by talking of earthly power. After all, King David had power, and this is what the people yearned for. But this talk of death had them baffled. How could a dead man seize a throne and rule a kingdom?

For us as for the disciples, prayer may come more easily when we have been successful. We like to talk to God when we have good things to tell him. We have shared our faith with someone; we have done a good deed; we have resisted a sharp temptation; then we pray. We feel good about ourselves and enjoy talking with God.

But when we feel anxious, almost helpless, as the disciples did, we hardly know how to pray. Our sense of failure crowds our desire to pray. Like a little child who shuns his daddy's gaze when he has done something wrong, we avoid God and seek refuge in sleep.

Their inability to recognize the true seriousness of their plight may have kept the disciples from praying. The mention of death undoubtedly made them anxious. You can imagine the uncertainty that clouded their minds as they heard the word. What would happen to them? They had left their families and jobs to follow Jesus. Now he was talking about leaving them. Yet grief and loneliness were not their real problems—compromise was.

The disciples' situation was serious—not because Christ was leaving but because they were in danger of selling out. Judas already had. Peter was facing pressure he couldn't take. The rest, except for John, were going to flee the scene of execution. And here in Gethsemane, the disciples who so often misunderstood their Master missed the point again. When they should have been wide awake in prayer, they were sound asleep.

We can learn from them. When you don't feel like praying, take a good look at your spiritual life. It may be worse than you would like to believe. One thing you can pray in such situations is "Lead us not into temptation, but deliver us from evil."

Christ's Concern
The Master is in charge to the very end. Even in the face of death he did not lose poise. The disciples had been careless, but their carelessness was more than matched by Christ's concern. The selflessness which had been his way of life stayed with him to the end. His chief concern was the welfare of his friends. The future of his program depended on them. He wanted to make sure that they were ready for the responsibilities he was passing on to them.

"Pray not for me, but for yourselves." If ever there was a time when Christ could have expected the support and encouragement of his friends, this was it. Yet it was his choice to minister to them rather than to urge them to minister to him. He practiced what he preached: "For the Son of man also came not to be served but to serve, and to give his life a ransom for many" (Mk 10:45).

61

Jesus knew he was ready to face his hour of suffering and death. It was for this that he came. But the disciples had not yet figured out what it was all about, and his concern was for them. These words of Christ's are comfortable ones to us. Whatever we go through, even our periods of prayerlessness, cannot stop the flow of his concern.

Be on guard against temptation. This was the second way that Christ's concern expressed itself in the midst of the disciples' carelessness. "Pray that you may not enter into temptation" (Lk 22:40). Their spiritual welfare rested heavily on his heart. Their steadfastness more than their safety was on his mind to the end. The large issues which would challenge the effectiveness of their future work for him were at stake. He wasted no time on peripheral matters. Sin or righteousness, obedience or rejection, success or failure were their choices. He urged them to pray that they would make the right ones.

Well he knew that the archenemy, Satan, who had failed to topple him in the beginning of his ministry, would be lying in wait for them at the end of that ministry. The baton was about to be passed from the Master to his followers, and it was a strategic time for Satan to trip them up.

Jesus' priorities are clear. And we would do well to heed them. We so often want happiness and comfort, security and success, appreciation and recognition—but Jesus is concerned with how we fare in temptation. If our righteousness and obedience are that important to him, we cannot afford to neglect to pray.

"Follow my example" was the other command

Christ gave his disciples at their moment of carelessness. His disciples were on his mind, and so undoubtedly was his mother. How would they get along without him? Especially heavy was the thought that he was to bear the sins of the whole world in his body on that cross.

Jesus had never known sin firsthand. Try as they would, his accusers could never point to sin in his life. Yet now the sins of the world were to be placed upon him. This was the cup that he had to drink, and he could taste its bitterness already. Still he prayed. And he calls each of us, whatever our lot, to follow his example. The Son of God could not live without prayer, and neither can you or I.

When it comes to prayer, feeling is not the most important thing. Feelings are fickle, easily influenced by health, morale, weather and mood. Prayer is too important to be put at the mercy of our feelings. "What if I don't feel like praying?" Plenty of God's people have felt the same way. Don't worry about it; pray anyway. Pray particularly that you may resist temptation, including the temptation not to pray.

The purpose of prayer is to maintain our relationship with God, not merely to express our feelings. This is why prayer is so important. Its purpose is not to ventilate our feelings but to celebrate our fellowship with God. We belong to God if we have met him through Jesus Christ. Nothing can take us out of God's hand. Our feelings cannot nullify the fact that God loves us and wants us to respond to his love. Prayer is one way we do this. As a good wife supports and encourages her husband even when she does not feel like it, we pray regularly in answer to God's constant love.

Christ's grace may be present even in the midst of our carelessness. Tenderly yet urgently he says to his drowsy disciples, "Why do you sleep? Rise and pray that you may not enter into temptation" (Lk 22:46). He knows what temptation is. He has just finished a sweaty struggle with it himself. And in his grace he reminds his friends that they will need more than their own resources to meet temptation head-on and defeat it.

He repeats the command he gave at the beginning. And the very repetition is an act of grace. Their failure to pray was not an irrecoverable, irreversible mistake. Christ's grace could take them beyond it. You may not have prayed for a long time, but Jesus' invitation still holds good. You have to do one thing only: start praying.

Lord, teach us to pray whether we feel like it or not. Teach us to pray especially when we don't feel like it. You know better than we the reasons why we have found it hard to pray. Help us not to get bogged down in them. We know that analysis of the problem is not the answer, but rather obedience to your command. Jesus not only urged us to pray, but he showed us how. We are grateful for him and all he means to us. He always gives us something to pray about. His love, his care, his call, his will, his purpose—teach us to pray about these and not to worry about our feelings. In his good name. Amen.

For further study of related themes refer to the following Scripture passages: Matthew 26:36-46; Mark 14:32-42; Hebrews 5:7-10.

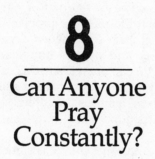

8

Can Anyone
Pray
Constantly?

PRAYER IS APPROPRIATE for special occasions. Prayer lends grace and dignity to our services and ceremonies. Buildings are dedicated, ships are launched, and public functions are opened with prayer. On these distinguished occasions, esteemed ministers, worthy bishops and learned rabbis are called upon to voice the sentiments of the citizenry in prayer. And it is proper to recognize God's presence on such occasions, as long as we don't deceive ourselves into thinking that he is always on our side or always approves of what we are doing.

Prayers seem especially fitting when we are in

trouble. During World War 2, reports circulated from the front lines indicated that there were no atheists in the foxholes. Passengers on a hijacked plane, office workers stranded in an elevator by a power failure, parents pacing the hospital corridor outside an operating room, athletes eager for the championship—all of these people may resort to prayer.

When we come to the end of our human resources, when life piles up problems faster than we can shovel them aside, when danger turns our palms sweaty and pushes our hearts into our mouths, we turn to prayer. After all, what else can we do? And it is obvious that we should pray in the midst of emergencies. Like Peter sinking in the water as he tried to walk toward Jesus, we too cry for help.

But if we think that prayer is something we do only in dignified ceremonies or desperate emergencies, we have missed its value. We treat prayer as though it were the spice of life, but the Bible prescribes it as a vital staple in our diet. We are content with a dash of praise, a pinch of petition, a drop of confession to bring a slight spiritual flavor to our secularity. We sprinkle a shake or two of the supernatural over our basic humanism and call the mixture religion. But God sees prayer as the breath of spiritual life.

To his friends at Thessalonica, Paul made this very clear. At the close of his first letter, he packed in a number of brief, pointed commands. Maybe he used the short phrase to make sure his readers could memorize these commands as the Jews had memorized the Ten Commandments. Anyway, as he often did, he brought his letter to an end in short, swift strokes. Among them is the terse command, "Pray constantly" (1 Thess 5:17).

This command cuts directly across the grain of our approach to prayer. We say, "Pray when the occasion deserves it," or "Pray when danger demands it." God says, "Pray constantly." "Wait a minute," we protest. "Do you mean I should pray continually?" That's exactly what the text says. "But my friends will write me off as a religious fanatic. Besides, if I pray all the time, how do I get anything else done? There are my job, my hobbies, my household tasks, my church responsibilities. All these need tending, and that leaves little time for praying."

But our protests are in vain. The commandment stands. The apostle's word is sure, based on the words of the Master himself: "And he told them a parable, to the effect that they ought always to pray and not lose heart" (Lk 18:1). Our task is not to get around the commandment but to understand it.

Context of the Command
God gives us a context within which his commandment makes sense, and that context is not nervousness or anxiety. We do not pray continually out of edginess about our relationship with God or our final destiny. Prayer is not a nervous habit that we engage in unconsciously like cracking our knuckles, tugging at our hair or biting our fingernails. Regular, spontaneous patterns of prayer do not stems from our fear that terrible things will happen

to us or our families if we do not pray.

Nor are guilt and despair our basic reasons for praying. Certainly we may pray out of desperation. When life figuratively sticks a gun in our ribs, backs us against a wall and snarls "Hands up!" we pray. And often our guilt drives us to prayer. Jesus, who knows us better than we know ourselves, taught us to pray, "And forgive us our debts,/As we also have forgiven our debtors" (Mt 6:12).

Prayer is not our neurotic response to difficult circumstances. It is not something we do in fitfulness or frenzy. Nor is it a compulsive concentration on our problem—as though all we did was squander our energies in telling God how bad life is. This kind of prayer life would sap our vitality like a low-grade infection. It would cause our spirits to shrivel in self-pity.

No, the context of the command is not nervousness or anxiety, guilt or despair, but joy and thanksgiving. The order to pray constantly is sandwiched between two words that ring with exuberance: "Rejoice always," and "Give thanks in all circumstances" (1 Thess 5:16, 18).

No grim and gloomy note here! No shuffling through life with bent back and tight brow. No colorless eking out an existence for which we have long since lost all relish!

But joy always: the confidence that the deep issues of life are settled, that God is alive and well and full of love, that my destiny is in his hands— and his are good hands. Not only joy always, but thanks in all circumstances. God is at work, and his is good work. We may not always choose or like what happens to us. But we can always trust God. No difficulty that we face can block his grace or nullify his love. Jesus' death on the cross is our guarantee of God's love. And so is the gift of God's own Spirit to all who stake their hopes on him. For whatever happens, then, we say, "Thanks."

Content of the Command

Joy and thanksgiving are the context of the command that tells us to pray constantly; what about the content of the command? Just what does Paul mean? He means for us to pray. He means for us to talk with God sincerely and personally as we go about our daily living. How many times as you work, play, drive, study, sew, cook, type, garden, do you find yourself carrying on silent conversation with an absent person? No one around you knows what you're thinking—and often that's a good thing. You may share some joy, review some problem, probe some secret, rebuke some fault, all without saying a word.

Prayer can be like this. God is a person, a person always present and always concerned. God the Holy Spirit is always in us and with us if we belong to Jesus. We don't have to find solitude to pray; neither do we have to use our voices or assume a certain posture. As we share our thoughts and feelings with God, we are praying.

Prayer is not only a specific activity which we engage in regularly; it is an attitude which we can reflect continually. A good way to describe this attitude is an awareness of the presence of God. Don't get me wrong. I'm not talking primarily about a feeling but about an assurance, a confident conviction that God is always with me, ready to hear my prayer.

I may not think about God every minute, but he is never far from my thoughts. This is what the command means. I may not be praying every second, but I'm always ready to pray at any moment. The word *constantly* (or as the King James Version has it, "without ceasing") is a good one to describe this experience of prayer. In an old Greek manuscript the word is used to describe a persistent cough—the kind of cough with which you are on the verge of coughing most of the time.

Consequences of the Command

So it is with prayer. The sense of God's presence makes it possible to pray anytime, anywhere. The spirit of prayer is part of our very lives. And when we live this way, certain consequences result.

First, *we open ourselves to God's will*. This life of joyful prayer is possible because we trust God's work in our lives. When we know he is working for our good, we are willing to obey. This grateful obedience is where life should have its center. Those who know and trust God in a relationship of prayer can take life as it comes because they know who is in charge. And they know that the ultimate outcome will be for their good.

With life immersed in prayer, we not only open ourselves to God's will, *we resist temptation*. Prayer does not eliminate temptation, but it helps. It reminds us of God's care. It warns us of sin's consequences. It links us to God's power.

One of the trustees of Fuller Theological Seminary was Herbert J. Taylor of Chicago. Dr. Charles Fuller invited Mr. Taylor to join the board when the seminary was founded in 1947, and he served with us until his death. His testimony was a tremendous help to me. Every day Mr. Taylor would spend an hour to an hour and a half reciting Scriptures that he had memorized. Many times he told me of the peace and joy that came from concentrating on God's Word and being conscious of his presence.

If you want to be fully human, you should pray continually. Nothing matures and develops our human potential more than fellowship with God. After all, that's what we were made for in the first place.

Our Father, forgive us for treating you like a dress suit that we only bring out on ceremonial occasions. Forgive us, too, for pretending that you are a fire extinguisher that we grab when things get hot. You are God. Help us to remember this and to share all of life with you. We know that this is the reasonable thing to do because you gave us life in the first place and then sent your Son to give us life again. We believe in prayer because we believe in you. Through our Lord Jesus we pray. Amen.

For further study of related themes refer to the following Scripture passages: Ephesians 5:20; 6:18; Philippians 4:4-7; Colossians 3:16-17; James 5:13-18.

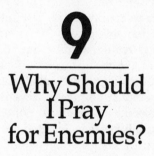

9

Why Should I Pray for Enemies?

FOR MOST OF US, the word *enemy* has almost dropped out of our vocabulary. When we do use it, it is usually limited to a military context. Even here we face confusion because the nations that were our enemies a generation ago have now become our allies. Yet I suppose all nations have enemies of some shade or other in this power-crazy, fear-filled world.

But we rarely use the word *enemy* to describe other persons or families in our circle of acquaintance. Stories of the conflict between Montague and Capulet in Shakespeare's *Romeo and Juliet* seem remote to us. So do the tales of feuding clans in the

Appalachians or battling tongs in Chinatown. The shoot-outs between good guys and bad guys in Western movies are at best historical curiosities and at worst tasteless episodes of violence and bloodletting.

The apparent armistice between individuals and families may be due more to apathy than to affection. It is possible that we don't care enough about each other to be openly angry. The antiseptic isolation of our urban living keeps us from building any kind of strong relationships, even hostile ones.

Sometimes we mask our true feelings toward others by rationalizing our relationship to them. Our deep personal animosity toward someone is called a personality conflict. In politics the candidate we would like to see defeated is called our opponent. In business the person whom we try to outdo is called our competitor. Of course, these relationships are not always antagonistic, but sometimes they are without our recognizing our true feelings.

Jesus, who knows our hearts much better than we do, took for granted that we would have enemies to deal with. And he made a point of helping us with this problem: "You have heard that it was said, 'You shall love your neighbor and hate your enemy.' But I say to you, Love your enemies and pray for those who persecute you" (Mt 5:43-44).

Those who first heard Jesus' words knew a lot about enemies and persecutors. The Egyptians before the exodus, the Philistines during the days of Saul and David, the Assyrians and Babylonians before the exile, the Persians during the exile, the

Seleucids under Antiochus Epiphanes, and more recently the Romans were all considered enemies and persecutors of the Jews. But the listeners were astonished at Jesus' command to love and pray for those who sought their harm.

This command surprises us too. We may not have open, sworn enemies, but we should not be naive about our hostilities. Psychologists have called our attention to the amount of anger many of us carry from childhood. Some of us release this hostility in wild ways like temper tantrums. Others express it in more subtle forms like cutting people with jokes or needling them with teasing. We are highly capable of being and making enemies.

In some cultures hostility toward Christians is direct and bitter. Among peoples who practice witchcraft, Christians may be blamed for natural disasters such as famine or flood. In lands where most people are Muslims, great pressure is brought to bear on any who depart from the faith of Muhammad and confess Jesus as the only Son of God. The command to pray on behalf of enemies has great import for them because they live among people who may literally plot against their lives.

But the command applies to us too. Wherever there are people who secretly rejoice in our failure, who consider us a threat to their welfare, who harbor ancient grudges, who resent our success, who reject our Christian witness, we have the makings of enemies. How we react to them may be a good indicator of our grasp of the Christian faith. Our Leader commanded us to pray for them in love and concern. And he meant just that.

Facing My Part

When we include prayer for our enemies in our prayer life, certain things begin to happen. First, we begin to face our responsibility for any misunderstandings that have arisen. Granted that the problem may be the other person's fault, we always have to check our own feelings and conduct to see how we could have handled it better. Reforming other people is not our job, but facing our own anger is. Our understanding of sin recognizes that whenever our relationships are strained, we are at least part culprit as well as victim.

Throughout this command to pray for those who persecute us, Jesus assumes that the hostility begins with the enemies. But we have to be sure it ends there and is not returned in kind. This is not easy when we are geared to retaliate. Praying may not completely cure our vindictiveness, but it will give us a good start on our way to recovery.

Seeing My Enemy as a Person

Praying for enemies will also help us to see them as individual persons. In our anxiety, resentment or anger, we are apt to see people who don't like us as threats to our security and objects to be feared or avoided. In our disappointment over their opposition, we are tempted mentally to dehumanize them. We tend to see only the aspects of conduct we resent. Praying for those who treat us wrongly reminds us that God made them, and nothing in their attitudes or conduct can nullify that.

The great danger in having enemies is not what they may do to us—it is what we do to ourselves as we allow harsh, bitter, angry reactions to develop. Our great temptation is to allow others' attitudes toward us to shape our attitudes. Thus we are in jeopardy of losing our freedom, of harboring ill feelings, of becoming what we don't want to be. Christ's plain command to pray for our enemies is a word of grace to protect us from ourselves.

When we voice our enemies' names and needs before God, we are leaving the final judgment to him. Our task is to pray; his is to judge. Only he knows the whole situation. Only he has the perspective to see all the issues and the wisdom to weigh them well. A person, whether enemy or not, deserves the fairest possible judgment. And that is God's responsibility, not mine.

Helping to Heal, Not Hurt

Life at best is sometimes a kind of friendly sparring, and at worst it becomes a knockdown, drag-out fight. Our natural tendency is to trade punch for punch. You snub me, and I ignore you. You blame me, and I'll toss the blame right back at you. Toe to toe we stand and slug it out. Praying for those who trouble us helps to break this cycle of vindictiveness. As we absorb hostility we dissipate its strength. And we may help to heal wounds, not aggravate them.

"Blessed are the peacemakers," Christ told his followers (Mt 5:9). Praying for our enemies can be our finest contribution to making peace with them.

Following My Father's Example

All of this is a prelude to Jesus' main point. To pray

for my enemies helps me face my part in the problem, see my enemy as a person and try to heal instead of hurt. To pray for my enemies also leads me to follow God's own example. Remember how Jesus phrased his command: "Love your enemies and pray for those who persecute you, so that you may be sons of your Father who is in heaven; for he makes his sun rise on the evil and on the good, and sends rain on the just and on the unjust" (Mt 5:44-45).

God treats well even those who are set against him. One way to show that we belong to him is to do the same. Grace is his way of life, and he calls us to live as he lives. "You, therefore, must be perfect, as your heavenly Father is perfect" (Mt 5:48). The same wholeness and maturity in love that are part of God's nature can be part of ours.

This is a practical command. It helps us cope with one of life's tough questions. It protects us from our foolish, frightful urge to be vindictive.

Above all, this is a Christian command. It lifts us above our ordinary ways of living, bound as we are to our race, class and culture. It links us to God's love which is so different from ours. It marks us as his children, ready to live on his terms.

Can I possibly pray for those whose aim is to make life impossible for me? For those who oppress my race, exploit my talents, resent my success, wish my hurt? Jesus told me I could. And he knows much more than I do. For one thing, he himself did just what he told us to do. All kinds of suffering dogged his path. Wherever he went, enemies sought his life. But even his dying words were concerned with their welfare, not their harm: "Father, forgive them; for they know not what they do" (Lk 23:34). That is true prayer—realistic, practical, Christian. We cannot do better than to follow his lead.

Our Heavenly Father, nowhere do we need your power more than right here. Loving our enemies and praying for those who persecute us are not our natural traits. Let it be your nature which controls us, not our own. Free us from the tyranny of theoretical praying, from the bondage of lip-service devotion. Let your powerful gospel make all the changes necessary to liberate us from our selfishness. Christ has commanded; help us to obey. In his lordly name. Amen.

For further study of related themes refer to the following Scripture passages: Leviticus 19:17-18; Matthew 6:12, 14-15; Luke 6:27-36; Romans 12:14-21.

10

Can I Be Completely Honest?

"YOU'RE NOT BEING honest." How often in one form or another do we hear these words? The young are especially sensitive to this matter of honesty. What they mean is not that people are lying to them, but that they don't reveal their true feelings.

Long conditioning has taught us to squelch and stifle some of what we feel. As children we learned that smiles are more acceptable than tears. We were encouraged to give compliments, not to issue complaints. When our dispositions were pleasant we received pats on the head. When our sourness showed itself we received swats on the other end. And most of us learned our lessons well: tell people what you think they want to hear, and don't reveal your negative feelings.

What we learn in our homes may affect our attitude toward God. After all, where do we first discover the meanings of trust, love, obedience, confession, forgiveness? We meet these in our family relationships long before we understand their spiritual meaning. Our attitudes toward life are formed by our contact with our earthly father well before we know what our heavenly Father is like. For many of us, it takes a while to sort out the difference. We may view God as an oversized projection of our human father.

If we have found it hard to be fully honest at home, we may find it hard to be honest with God. This is one of our basic problems in prayer. Almost unconsciously we feel that we should tell God what he wants to hear, not what we really think. Two things happen when we do this. First, our prayers become dishonest; we play games with God, mouthing nice words and smothering our awkward thoughts. Second, we may stop praying. If we can only talk to God about good things, what happens to prayer when everything goes bad? We have no appetite for it. To mutter pleasant sounds from a spirit full of bitterness is a mockery. So prayer ceases.

Can I really be honest with God? We have it on God's own word that we can. In the Bible God himself has preserved for us examples of honesty in prayer, honesty that is stinging in its candor. Job, Psalms, Habakkuk and especially Jeremiah are cases in point. Jeremiah begins a prayer: "Right-

eous art thou, O LORD, when I complain to thee,
yet I would plead my case before thee" (Jer 12:1).
An accurate paraphrase of these words would
run something like this: "When I argue with you,
you are always right. But I'm going to argue anyway."

Jeremiah's complaint before God was based on
God's seeming silence in the face of blatant injustice. "Why does the way of the wicked prosper?
Why do all who are treacherous thrive?" (Jer 12:1).
In other words, Jeremiah had a basic disagreement
with God over the way he was running the universe. And he did not hesitate to tell God this.

Chapter twenty of Jeremiah records an even
sharper protest. "O LORD, thou hast deceived me,
and I was deceived; thou art stronger than I, and
thou hast prevailed. I have become a laughingstock
all the day; every one mocks me" (Jer 20:7). I have
been to a lot of prayer meetings in my day, but
I have never heard anyone begin a prayer like that!
That's honesty of a high order, frank and refresh-
ing.

Living with Our Problems
Let's be careful to understand what happened: Jeremiah's honest prayer did not cure his problems,
but it did help him to live with them.

The circumstances that made him so distraught
had not changed. The political situation was as
confusing as ever. The king of Judah continued on
his merry way, heedless of Jeremiah's warnings
not to rebel against Nebuchadnezzar and the Babylonians. The priests were still dead set against Jere-

miah because of his dire prophecies about the destruction of the Temple. His own family was still deeply embarrassed at his outspoken indictments of the political and religious establishments.

God, himself, was still puzzlingly slow in doing what he had promised. God was prompting Jeremiah to prophesy judgment, and then no judgment took place. The prophet felt like a fool, and his enemies took great comfort in his loss of face. "I have become a laughingstock all the day; every one mocks me. For whenever I speak, I cry out, I shout, 'Violence and destruction!' For the word of the LORD has become for me a reproach and derision all day long" (Jer 20:7-8).

The hallmark of the true prophet was that his prophecy was fulfilled. God himself had established this proof of a prophet's genuineness when he set up the prophetic office in the book of Deuteronomy: "And if you say in your heart, 'How may we know the word which the LORD has not spoken?' —when a prophet speaks in the name of the LORD, if the word does not come to pass or come true, that is a word which the LORD has not spoken; the prophet has spoken it presumptuously, you need not be afraid of him" (Deut 18:21-22).

You can feel Jeremiah's predicament. God had commanded him to proclaim judgment, and Jeremiah faithfully obeyed. In fact, he had no choice. "If I say, 'I will not mention him, or speak any more in his name,' there is in my heart as it were a burning fire shut up in my bones, and I am weary with holding it in, and I cannot" (Jer 20:9). What he prophesies does not come true, yet God will not let him quit. The end result is appallingly clear. God had made Jeremiah appear a false prophet in the eyes of his own people.

Here's his description of their reactions: "For I hear many whispering. Terror is on every side! 'Denounce him! Let us denounce him!' say all my familiar friends, watching for my fall. 'Perhaps he will be deceived, then we can overcome him, and take our revenge on him' " (Jer 20:10).

But the important thing is that Jeremiah takes his plight directly to God. The external circumstances may not have changed, but the internal pressure is relieved. He has taken his problem out of the dark depths of his own spirit and bared it to the light of God's love and power. No more festering, no more irrational fear or unreasonable anger. A problem, yes! But a problem that is being faced and expressed.

Fuming, fretting or fussing is not the answer to our deep difficulties, confusion about God's will or resentment of God's ways. Prayer is. Frankly, openly, directly, telling God how we feel will help us live with our problems as Jeremiah lived with his.

Expressing Our Trust in God

But honest prayer does much more than that. It is actually an expression of our trust in God. Think of the people you know with whom you are willing to share your secrets. They are people whom you trust. A wise colleague of mine once defined a friend as "someone with whom you can be weak." Only with those whom we trust will we share our real selves, including those parts of our disposition we wish were different.

Jeremiah's honesty with God was not hypocrisy. He did not pretend to be honest while spewing up false problems or concocting phony questions in order to keep God at a distance. His honest prayers flowed from his desire to know God better and to trust him more. Like the man in the Gospel story, he prayed, "I believe; help my unbelief!" (Mk 9:24).

In the midst of his confusion, Jeremiah retained his confidence. "But the LORD is with me as a dread warrior; therefore my persecutors will stumble, they will not overcome me" (Jer 20:11). This is a secure relationship unrattled by conflict, disagreement and uncertainty. Jeremiah has no other God, no other refuge. He is not always pleased with what God does, but his trust is so strong he can share even his discomfort in prayer.

Strengthening Our Sense of Call
At the beginning of his ministry, Jeremiah had been called by God to preach. He was a young man —too young, he thought, to shoulder a prophet's weighty responsibilities. God's answer was blunt: "Do not say, 'I am only a youth'; for to all to whom I send you you shall go, and whatever I command you you shall speak. Be not afraid of them, for I am with you to deliver you, says the LORD" (Jer 1:7-8).

Jeremiah found this sense of call inescapable. As with him, so with us—call and conflict go hand in hand. Doing the will of God is not always easy. Interpreting the ways of God to the world is not only difficult, it can be downright unpleasant. God's actions may mystify us; his words are frequently baffling.

But as we tell God our doubts and misunderstandings, three things happen. First, our problems take on a clearer perspective. They no longer are left lurking in the gloomy recesses of our insides where they continue to reinfect us with resentment or self-pity.

Second, our relationship with God and our sense of call are strengthened. As we are honest with him, we come to know him better and to love him more.

Third, honesty with God means we can pray in all circumstances. God wants to hear what we have to say; we don't have to guess what he wants to hear. He takes us as we are. He can accept our negative feelings as well as our praise, our questions as well as our gratitude. After all, he knows our hearts; what can we possibly hide from him?

"Can I really be honest with God?" Surely, because good men and women have shown us the way. In all of life, honesty is the best policy. With God it is the only one.

Thank you, Father, for encouraging us to be ourselves. Thank you for giving us examples of those who trusted you when they were baffled by you. Sometimes we feel this way and are afraid or ashamed to tell you. Forgive us for not remembering that you are our Father, open to all our prayers, responsive to all our needs—even our need to tell you things we don't like. Your love at such times is especially comforting to us. Let it shine through our distress and brighten our knowledge of you. Through Jesus Christ. Amen.

For further study of related themes refer to the following Scripture passages: Job 3:1-3; 32:17-22; Proverbs 8:6-9.

How
Can I
Pray More?

WE HAVE GRAPPLED with many problems that hinder our prayers, but the last problem is at once the hardest and the simplest: How can I pray more? Prayer—conversation with God—is so much harder than conversation with another human being. In prayer we don't see a face; we don't hear an audible voice; we don't feel a physical touch. Clear answers often come slowly, when they come at all.

Yet if prayer gives us problems, reluctance to pray and lack of prayer cause greater problems.

Almost any of us will pray when the occasion demands. We may be asked to give thanks for food at the home of a friend who knows our Christian commitment. We may be asked to lead in prayer for the offering in our Sunday-school class. At prayer meeting the pastor may call on us to voice a special request for a financial problem or a sick missionary. It may be halting and tense, but we do pray, and I am sure that the Lord values such prayers.

Or let an emergency pinch us sharply enough, and we begin to pray. Business turns sour, and we are working day and night to stave off bankruptcy. Cancer strikes a loved one, and we wonder what the surgeon's scalpel will uncover. A teen-ager runs away from home, and we wait anxiously for the phone to ring. Prayer becomes vitally important at such times, and I'm sure God wants us to call upon him when we experience need.

We also pray when we happen to feel like it. An old spiritual declares, "Every time I feel the Spirit moving in my heart I will pray." But we cannot afford to relegate prayer to the control of our feelings. When I don't feel the Spirit moving in my heart, can I safely neglect prayer?

The Bible tells us that prayer should be a carefully developed habit as well as a spontaneous expression. This double role can be illustrated in the lives of athletes. I can recall Willie Mays virtually climbing the outfield fence in a baseball game to clutch a towering drive just before it left the park. He tumbled in a heap with another outfielder but held the ball for the out. It was a superb play at a crucial spot, and it was only possible because of the sound training habits Willie had followed through the years. He kept himself trim; his reflexes were sharp; his natural instincts were honed to a fine edge by countless hours of practice. He made the big play because he had been faithfully executing the ordinary plays along the way. He was in the habit of playing well.

Our muscles need toning even if we are not athletes. Just walking, climbing stairs and bending over to do our chores require good conditioning. Spend a couple of weeks in bed and you find that out in a hurry. Engage in a few hours of heavy gardening after a winter's layoff and you discover muscles you forgot you had. We should continually discipline our bodies even if we are not athletes.

Anything worth doing requires practice and conditioning. Prayer is no exception. If we are disciplined and dedicated in prayer, we will be ready for the emergencies and challenges that call for power and wisdom in prayer. How can we develop habits of prayer? A look at the experiences of the prophet-statesman Daniel will be of help to us. In the famous lion's den story two lessons stand out that will encourage us as we learn to pray.

Realize Prayer Is Essential
Daniel had been appointed one of three presidents whom King Darius had set up over his Persian empire. And the king had even greater plans for Daniel: "Then this Daniel became distinguished above all the other presidents and satraps, because an excellent spirit was in him; and the king planned to set him over the whole kingdom" (Dan 6:3).

Daniel's upcoming promotion set the stage for jealousy and a dramatic conflict. The other officials searched desperately for defects in Daniel's performance, but "he was faithful, and no error or fault was found in him" (6:4). They finally hatched a plot that would discredit Daniel because of his religious practices. They persuaded the king to establish a law which banned all prayer except petitions to the king of Persia himself.

The new law did not deter Daniel. "When Daniel knew that the document had been signed, he went to his house where he had windows in his upper chamber open toward Jerusalem; and he got down upon his knees three times a day and prayed and gave thanks before his God, as he had done previously. Then these men came by agreement and found Daniel making petition and supplication before his God" (6:10-11).

Daniel's prayer schedule shows how indispensable he believed prayer to be. Thanksgiving, petition and supplication formed the pattern of his praying. Thanking God for special blessings and asking for special help were prominent elements. These appeared in Daniel's praying because they were essential ingredients in his living.

Daniel knew, as we all know, that many blessings come our way which we do not earn. None of us get only what we deserve. In the midst of great suffering, a man of deep faith affirmed, "The steadfast love of the LORD never ceases, his mercies never come to an end; they are new every morning; great is thy faithfulness" (Lam 3:22-23). If we really believe that God gives us many good things beyond our deserving, thanksgiving will be frequently expressed.

So will petition and supplication. Daniel knew,

as we must, that problems beyond our capability are daily experiences. Our status quo is a kind of constant crisis. Human resources run thin; our energies flag; our minds stagger at the size of our problems; our emotions stretch tight on the rack of anxious relationships. Pray we must, if we are to conquer circumstances, asking God regularly to intervene and change the situation or give us the strength and courage to accept it. Prayer is not an option for people who want victory; life demands prayer.

Daniel's persistence in prayer proves its importance to him. He was not a wild revolutionary, but a highly responsible officer of the land, staunchly committed to the laws of the empire. But prayer prohibition was a law he had to break.

Prayer was so central to Daniel's devotion to God that nothing could take its place. He did not rationalize by claiming that his inner attitude was what counted: "After all, I can pray secretly in my heart, and the king's men will never be wiser." Prayer-allegiance to God could not be compromised.

Set Definite Times for Prayer

Prayer was not something Daniel did on the run. His example is significant for us. He set aside a regular place for prayer, the upper chamber with its windows open toward Jerusalem, the city that symbolized God's presence with his people. He assumed a regular posture in prayer, down on his knees in contrition and concentration. He followed a regular schedule of prayer, three times a day, according to Jewish custom. The great Old Testament creed—"Hear, O Israel: The LORD our God is one LORD" (Deut 6:4)—was traditionally repeated morning, noon and night. God had commanded this: "And [you] shall talk of them [these words] when you sit in your house, and when you walk by the way, and when you lie down, and when you rise" (Deut 6:7).

Daniel's example carries suggestions for us. Morning prayer is a time for praise and thanksgiving. The great hymns of the church have recognized this. "When morning gilds the skies, my heart awaking cries, 'May Jesus Christ be praised.'" Or, "Holy, Holy, Holy, Lord God Almighty! Early in the morning our song shall rise to thee." Let praise in the morning become a way of life for you. Thank God for health and safety, home and friends, strength to work or grace to suffer. "Praise God, from whom all blessings flow." Then commit your day to his loving care. Ask God to guide your steps, guard your words, strengthen your love, encourage your heart. Let no day begin without these conscious expressions of praise and commitment.

Let no day end without confession and intercession. Make it a habit to review each day and to ask God to forgive what you have mishandled or misspoken. Quiet reflection on the course of every day's activities can help prevent the repetition of mistakes. I have found this time profitable for recalling the people I have met or talked to during the day and to mention them specifically in prayer. This habit will keep our prayers from becoming ingrown and self-centered.

During the day, let circumstances guide your

prayers. Deal with problems prayerfully as you meet them. Share them quickly and quietly with God. When you think of the name of a friend or Christian worker, be specific. Pray for his or her needs on the spot. Morning, evening and during the day let your voice join with the church of God around the earth and the hosts in heaven, praising and petitioning your Maker and Redeemer.

Like Patrick Henry, who reduced life's great options to "liberty or death," Daniel confronted the king's men with his commitment to prayer or death. If real life hinges on prayer, the choice is clear-cut for both Daniel and for us.

Father, lead us to a constancy in prayer that is a worthy reflection of your constancy in love and grace. We know that our prayers do not earn your favor. But we also know that prayer is our fitting response to the favor you have already shown us in Jesus. Help us dare to be Daniels, fervent in devotion, courageous in prayer. Through Jesus Christ's good name, we pray. Amen.

For further study of related themes refer to the following Scripture passages: Matthew 6:6-15; 14:23; Mark 6:46; Luke 18:1; 2 Thessalonians 1:11.

264.1
H83
1983

111458

LINCOLN CHRISTIAN COLLEGE AND SEMINARY

3 4711 00196 3299